Family Fun
for Easter

Barnabas
for
Children®

Barnabas for Children® is a registered word mark and the logo is a registered device mark
of The Bible Reading Fellowship

Text copyright © Jane Butcher 2011
Illustrations copyright © Mark Brierley 2011
The author asserts the moral right
to be identified as the author of this work

Published by
The Bible Reading Fellowship
15 The Chambers, Vineyard
Abingdon OX14 3FE
United Kingdom
Tel: +44 (0)1865 319700
Email: enquiries@brf.org.uk
Website: www.brf.org.uk
BRF is a Registered Charity

ISBN 978 0 85746 049 3

First published 2011
10 9 8 7 6 5 4 3 2 1 0
All rights reserved

Acknowledgments
Unless otherwise stated, scripture quotations are taken from the Contemporary English
Version of the Bible published by HarperCollins Publishers, copyright © 1991, 1992, 1995
American Bible Society.

Pages 14–15: Bread dough recipe taken from *Messy Church 2*, p. 71
Page 31: Basic biscuit dough recipe taken from *Messy Cooks*, p. 17
Page 35: Passover meal idea extended from *Messy Church*, pp. 159–60
Page 45: Empty-tomb rolls recipe taken from *Messy Cooks*, p. 100

A catalogue record for this book is available from the British Library

Printed in Singapore by Craft Print International Ltd

The paper used in the production of this publication was supplied by mills that source their
raw materials from sustainably managed forests. Soy-based inks were used in its printing
and the laminate film is biodegradable.

**30 Lent and Easter activities
for families to share**

Jane Butcher

To Katie for her creative ideas and Ruth Brooker for her willingness to test them

Contents

Foreword

No time of the year is as rich spiritually as the weeks leading up to Easter. And no time has as much potential for engaging children in the key events of their faith. But the wonderful build-up and climax to the season can be so easily missed if it isn't entered into day by day. Jane Butcher has written a lovely, easy guide to Easter celebration, including Lent, Mother's Day and Holy Week. No family can fail to enjoy the fun of establishing traditions, old and new, that will make the Easter story come alive in their home.

Michele Guinness

Introduction

'Easter' is not just about the school holidays or the bank holiday weekend, although both can be very enjoyable. It's also not just about chocolate eggs and bunny rabbits, even though it may sometimes seem that way in the media or at your child's school. Sometimes the pressure—on our children and from our children—to turn Easter into a chocolate fest can seem overwhelming. Has Easter become all about spending and consuming, or can it be reclaimed as something more positive and more meaningful? Is it possible to rediscover the essence of Easter?

Well, the run-up to Easter starts a month or so earlier with the season of Lent. Over the years a number of traditional customs have sprung up, providing lots of opportunities for families to enjoy fun activities together over the weeks leading up to Easter. It's also a great way to mark the change from winter and Christmas to the new season of spring, and for Christians it gives the opportunity to recognise the importance of Lent and the celebration of Easter Sunday.

This book offers thirty ideas for activities to share as a family right through the season of Lent, starting with Shrove Tuesday, up to Holy Week and Easter Day itself. There are also suggestions for things to talk about and think about with your children along the way. I hope you have lots of family fun this Easter!

Jane Butcher

What is Lent?

Lent is the 40 days before Easter. In case you or your children try to count the days, it is helpful to know that the six Sundays are not included! Lent reminds us of the 40 days that Jesus spent in the wilderness, getting ready for his ministry. Traditionally, it has been seen as a time of denial—maybe giving up something. Different people will choose different ways to mark the season.

Many people do choose to give up something for Lent, and this is a significant decision. Whether it's chocolate or wine or a favourite activity, these things that we really enjoy aren't necessarily wrong in themselves, but the act of giving something up for a period of time can be a way of coming closer to God. It helps to remind us of all the things that we don't really need, and that we rely on God for everything. It can help us to be more aware of temptation and of our need for God's help in resisting temptation. It can also help us to appreciate the gifts we have when parts of the world have so little.

Others may choose to 'do' something rather than giving something up. This may be to set aside a regular amount of time each day to help others or to spend some time with God, perhaps by sharing some Lent reading together or praying together. There are some very good books published by Barnabas that you could share with your children during Lent and Easter. A list can be found on pages 54 and 55.

Lent can also be a time to think about and say sorry for the things we have done wrong.

It can help children to understand more about the purpose of Lent if you talk about it being a time of 'getting ready' to celebrate the festival of Easter, just as Advent is a time of 'getting ready' to celebrate the festival of Christmas.

With your children, **talk about** why we mark Lent. Ask them what Easter means to them. The answer may well be 'chocolate eggs', but you may find as you move through Lent to Easter that the activities in this book inspire new thoughts—both for yourself and your children.

Temptation!

It's hard to give things up, and very tempting to 'give up' in the wrong way after a few days! Read the story of Jesus in the wilderness with your children to see how he dealt with 40 days of temptation.

1. Read Matthew's Gospel, chapter 4, verses 1 to 11

The Holy Spirit led Jesus into the desert, so that the devil could test him. After Jesus had gone without eating for forty days and nights, he was very hungry. Then the devil came to him and said, 'If you are God's Son, tell these stones to turn into bread.' Jesus answered, 'The Scriptures say:

"No one can live only on food. People need every word that God has spoken."'

Next, the devil took Jesus to the holy city and had him stand on the highest part of the temple. The devil said, 'If you are God's Son, jump off. The Scriptures say:

"God will give his angels orders about you. They will catch you in their arms, and you won't hurt your feet on the stones."'

Jesus answered, 'The Scriptures also say:

"Don't try to test the Lord your God!"'

Finally, the devil took Jesus up on a very high mountain and showed him all the kingdoms on earth and their power. The devil said to him, 'I will give all this to you, if you will bow down and worship me.'

Jesus answered, 'Go away, Satan! The Scriptures say:

"Worship the Lord your God and serve only him."'

Then the devil left Jesus, and angels came to help him.

2. Egg and spoon obstacle courses

Try one or more of these temptation-themed challenges!

Jesus was tempted by the devil to step off the right path, but he knew he needed to trust God and stay on the right path. Set out an obstacle course in the house or garden. It could be some sturdy furniture, cushions, boxes, hula hoops or anything safe that is close at hand. Each person has to walk through the course as quickly as possible without the egg falling off the spoon.

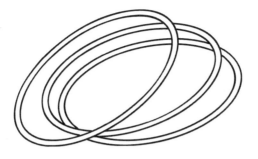

To make it a little harder:

Set up an obstacle course as before. Each person has to walk the course as quickly as possible holding a cardboard tube with a small chocolate egg inside. Hold it flat to stop the egg from falling out.

To make it even harder, replace the egg with a marble!

3. Plaited bread

One temptation Jesus faced in the desert was to turn stones into bread. This bread-making activity is both enjoyable and thought-provoking.

First, make the bread dough.

You will need:

400g strong plain flour
2 level tsp sugar
2 level tsp dried yeast (the easy baking variety)
230ml plus 5 tbsp warm water
1.5 level tsp salt
2 tbsp olive oil

1. Sift the flour, sugar, yeast and salt into a bowl. (If you are using yeast that needs to be reconstituted in water first, follow the instructions on the packet.)

2. Add the oil and water and knead well.

3. Cover with a clean tea towel and leave in a warm place for approximately one hour until doubled in size.

4. Divide the dough into three pieces and roll the pieces into long strands to represent the three temptations Jesus faced.

5. Plait the bread and bake in the oven at 190°C or Gas Mark 5 for 45–50 minutes until the top is golden brown and the base sounds hollow when tapped.

6. Cool on a wire rack.

When you eat it together, **talk about** the things that tempt you the most.

Note: If you are short of time, you could use a shop-bought bread mix.

Shrove Tuesday

The day before Lent starts is Shrove Tuesday, commonly known as 'Pancake Day'. 'Shrove' means 'your sins are forgiven'. Many years ago, people would go to church on this day to be shriven—to confess their sins and receive forgiveness. Because Lent would be a time when people would eat less or even fast from food completely, pancakes were a way of using up all the flour, eggs and milk in the house before Lent started.

4. Shrove Tuesday project

Talk about the tradition of Shrove Tuesday, and set a little project for the children to find out what other countries call this day. For example, in France it is known as Mardi Gras—Fat Tuesday!

5. Pancake party

Have a pancake party with family and friends.

You may have your own favourite pancake recipe, but if not, you could try this one.

You will need:

110g plain flour
A pinch of salt
2 eggs
275ml milk
50g butter

1. Sift the flour and salt into a large mixing bowl. Make a well in the centre of the flour and break the eggs into it. Then begin whisking the mixture. Any sort of whisk or even a fork will do.

2. Next, gradually add the milk, still whisking. When the mixture is the consistency of thin cream, melt the butter in a pan. Spoon two tablespoons of the melted butter into the batter and whisk it in. Use the rest to grease the pan, using a small piece of kitchen paper to smear it round before you make each pancake.

3. Get the pan really hot. Then turn the heat down to medium. Spoon some batter into the hot pan—just enough to cover the base of the pan (using a ladle if you have one). As soon as the batter is in the pan, tip it around from side to side to get the base evenly coated with batter. It should take only half a minute or so to cook; you can lift the edge with a palette knife to see if it's tinged golden brown as it should be. Flip the pancake over—the other side will need a few seconds only—then slide it out of the pan onto a plate.

4. Stack the pancakes as you make them between sheets of greaseproof paper on a plate fitted over a pan of simmering water, or in a low oven, to keep them warm while you make the rest.

5. Top with your favourite toppings—sweet or savoury—the choice is yours!

Note: An alternative for those who don't like pancakes is to buy some plain pizza bases and top with your favourite toppings.

Ash Wednesday

Lent starts on Ash Wednesday. Ashes are a very old symbol of mourning and repentance, and in some churches they are still used in the service on Ash Wednesday. Traditionally, the ash is made by burning the leftover palm crosses from the previous year (see **Palm Sunday**, pages 28–31), then mixed with a little water.

6. Attend a service

The minister uses the ash to make the sign of the cross on each person's forehead, as a symbol of our need for Jesus in our lives. You may feel that this is a strange custom, but children are often keen to take part in it if they have the opportunity.

7. Lenten resolution

Talk about why this day gets its name, and encourage everyone in your family to make a Lenten resolution. This could be something that you do to help others, for example, giving a regular amount of money to a particular charity or cause. One way in which you could do this as a family, if you are financially able, is to agree which charity or cause you will support during Lent, put a suitable pot on your table, and make a contribution at the main meal of each day. If your children have money of their own, they can be encouraged to give a small amount themselves. If this is not appropriate, it can still be valuable that they see their parents doing this, even if it is just a small amount.

Spring activities

8. Easter garden

It's worth making this early on in Lent, so that it is ready in time for Easter Sunday.

1. Get a large tray or container and put soil in the base.

2. Sink in a plant pot on its side to create the tomb in which Jesus was laid.

3. Decorate some large stones and add to the garden.

4. Find a large stone to cover the mouth of the tomb, but do not place it in position yet. This is a task for Good Friday, the day when Jesus died and was placed in the tomb.

5. Make three crosses from sticks and stand them in the soil.

6. You could add pebbles to make a path, and some twigs for trees, or plant some cress seeds in time for them to have started growing by Easter Sunday.

9. Plant some seeds

You could also plant some seeds in the garden, in a window box or in pots. This helps us to think about the death of Jesus and his burial. When the seeds start to shoot and grow, you can then also **talk about** the new life that has come from the seeds that were buried in the ground.

Mothering Sunday

Mothering Sunday is the fourth Sunday in Lent. Traditionally it was a day when people could take a break from the seriousness of Lent. The tradition of calling this particular day Mothering Sunday goes back to Roman times when, as the Christian church spread, there developed the pattern of honouring the Church as a mother figure. From this, there developed the tradition of children honouring their mothers on this day. Youngsters who worked away from home were allowed to go and visit their mothers on Mothering Sunday, and they may have taken a Simnel cake as a gift.

10. Make a Simnel cake

A Simnel cake is a fruit cake with a layer of marzipan and eleven marzipan eggs on the top, symbolising eleven of Jesus' disciples. (The missing twelfth egg stands for Judas Iscariot, who betrayed Jesus.) An easy way of making a Simnel cake is to use a shop-bought fruit cake and some marzipan.

1. Roll out the marzipan to a size that will cover the top of the cake, leaving enough to make eleven small balls or egg shapes.

2. Melt some marmalade or apricot jam in a saucepan and brush over the top of the fruit cake.

3. Lay the marzipan on top.

4. Make eleven balls from the leftover marzipan, and put them around the edge of the top of the cake.

5. Brown lightly under the grill.

Note: Marzipan contains ground almonds, so it is not suitable for anyone with a nut allergy.

Holy Week

Holy Week is the week leading up to Easter Sunday. Some of the days in this week have special names because of the events that happened in the week before the first Easter.

Palm Sunday

The Sunday before Easter is known as Palm Sunday. It celebrates when Jesus arrived in Jerusalem, riding on a donkey, for the Jewish festival of Passover.

Maundy Thursday

This is when the Last Supper took place. Jesus shared a meal with his disciples. He also shared bread and wine with them. It was at this meal that Jesus said that one of the disciples would turn against him and betray him, which Judas then did.

Good Friday

This is when Jesus was arrested and put on trial. He was nailed on a cross, where he died. This is known as crucifixion. His body was then wrapped in cloths and placed in a tomb.

Easter Saturday

This is the day when Jesus rested in the grave.

Easter Sunday

This is not part of Holy Week, but a new beginning! It is the day when Christians celebrate that Jesus rose from the dead. When some of Jesus' friends went back to the tomb, they found that it was empty. Only the empty cloths that Jesus had been wrapped in were left.

Holy Week: Palm Sunday

Palm Sunday is the first day of Holy Week. It's the day when we remember Jesus riding into Jerusalem. Crowds came out to cheer him, wave palm branches and lay down their cloaks on the ground.

11. Read Mark's Gospel, chapter 11, verses 1 to 11

When they were getting close to Jerusalem, Jesus sent two of them on ahead. He told them, 'Go into the next village. As soon as you enter it, you will find a young donkey that has never been ridden. Untie the donkey and bring it here. If anyone asks why you are doing that, say, "The Lord needs it and will soon bring it back." '

The disciples left and found the donkey tied near a door that faced the street. While they were untying it, some of the people standing there asked, 'Why are you untying the donkey?' They told them what Jesus had said, and the people let them take it.

The disciples led the donkey to Jesus. They put some of their clothes on its back, and Jesus got on. Many people spread clothes on the road, while others went to cut branches from the fields.

In front of Jesus and behind him, people went along shouting,

'Hooray! God bless the one who comes in the name of the Lord! God bless the coming kingdom of our ancestor David. Hooray for God in heaven above!'

After Jesus had gone to Jerusalem, he went into the temple and looked around at everything. But since it was already late in the day, he went back to Bethany with the twelve disciples.

12. Palm crosses

If you are given palm crosses at church on Palm Sunday, bring them home and arrange them in a display. Alternatively, write on the date and use them as bookmarks, perhaps in a Bible. Children could use theirs as markers in their children's Bibles.

13. Pin the tail on the donkey

Take turns, wearing a blindfold, to pin the tail on the donkey. You can buy this game, print one from the internet or draw your own. You could use string, wool or a tie with sticky tape attached as the tail.

14. Palm Sunday biscuits

You will need:

200g self-raising flour
100g caster sugar
100g butter
1 beaten egg
(replace with a small
amount of milk if
preferred)

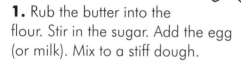

1. Rub the butter into the
flour. Stir in the sugar. Add the egg
(or milk). Mix to a stiff dough.

2. Knead the dough lightly and
then place on a floured surface.

3. Roll out to a thickness of 5mm.
Cut into leaf shapes.

4. Use a palette knife to transfer the biscuits to a baking
tray lined with greaseproof paper.

5. Bake at 200°C or Gas Mark 6 for 10–15 minutes.

6. Allow to cool on the tray before serving.

Holy Week: Maundy Thursday

Maundy Thursday is the day before Good Friday. On this day, we remember the Last Supper that Jesus shared with his disciples. 'Maundy' comes from a Latin word which means 'a command', and it refers to Jesus' command that he gave at the Last Supper, that we should love one another as he loves us. At the Last Supper, Jesus washed his disciples' feet, and offered them the bread and the wine as signs of his body and blood, which would be given for us through his death.

15. Read Mark's Gospel, chapter 14, verses 17 to 25

While Jesus and the twelve disciples were eating together that evening, he said, 'The one who will betray me is now eating with me.'

This made the disciples sad, and one after another they said to Jesus, 'You surely don't mean me!' He answered, 'It is one of you twelve men who is eating from this dish with me. The Son of Man will die, just as the Scriptures say. But it is going to be terrible for the one who betrays me. That man would be better off if he had never been born.'

During the meal Jesus took some bread in his hands. He blessed the bread and broke it. Then he gave it to his disciples and said, 'Take this. It is my body.'

Jesus picked up a cup of wine and gave thanks to God. He gave it to his disciples, and they all drank some. Then he said, 'This is my blood, which is poured out for many people, and with it God makes his agreement. From now on I will not drink any wine, until I drink new wine in God's kingdom.'

16. Passover meal

The first Passover is described in the book of Exodus, chapter 12, when the Israelites were slaves in Egypt. One lamb was killed for each Israelite household, and the blood was painted on the doorposts. This would be a sign to the angel of death to 'pass over' the house and not kill the oldest boy in the family. The family were to eat the lamb, bitter herbs and unleavened bread— which is flat bread that has no yeast—before they left Egypt to go to the Promised Land. God said that every year the children of Israel should celebrate this festival to remember when they were saved from slavery in Egypt.

This is the festival that Jesus and his disciples were celebrating at the Last Supper, and this is the meal that is eaten on Maundy Thursday.

The Passover meal was a special family occasion, and can be adapted for your family.

You will need:

A small bowl of horseradish sauce
A small bowl of salt water
A small bowl of *haroseth* (date paste) or apple sauce
Some cooked lamb
A matzo or pitta bread
Wine or grape juice
A large white candle

Place all the items on the table and light the candle. Read out the following traditional questions and answers for this meal time.

Question: Why do we have bitter herbs to eat today?

Answer: The bitter herbs (horseradish sauce) remind us of the bitterness of slavery. They remind us of when God's people were slaves in Egypt long, long ago.

Question: Why is there salt water to taste today?

Answer: The salt water reminds us of the tears God's people cried when they were slaves in Egypt.

Question: Why have we got this haroseth paste today?

Answer: This sauce reminds us of the mud that God's people had to use to make bricks when they were slaves in Egypt.

Question: Why have we got lamb to eat today?

Answer: The lamb reminds us of the lamb's blood that protected the houses of God's people in Egypt, so that the angel of death passed over them and didn't hurt their eldest sons. It also reminds us that Jesus is the Lamb of God who died for us on Good Friday so that we could be friends with God.

Question: Why have we got flat bread to eat today?

Answer: The bread reminds us of the way God rescued his people from Egypt. They had to leave in such a hurry that there was no time for the bread to rise. It also reminds us that Jesus took bread at his Passover meal and gave it to his friends saying, 'Eat this, this is my body given for you. Do this to remember me.'

Question: Why do we drink wine today?

Answer: The wine reminds us of God's blessing, when he rescued his people from Egypt and took them to a land full of good things. It also reminds us that at the

Passover meal Jesus took a cup of wine and said, 'This is my blood, poured out for you. Do this to remember me.' As people taste the foods in turn, choose from the words 'like', 'don't like', 'don't mind'. Alternatively, you could have a list and place a tick, cross or question mark next to each item.

Finally someone says, 'We eat this food today to remember God's rescue of his people at Passover and at Easter time, and the way he still guides us today. Let's give thanks to God together.'

Holy Week: Good Friday

After the Passover meal, Jesus went out with his friends to the Garden of Gethsemane on the Mount of Olives. It was night-time. He knew that Judas would tell the soldiers where he was, and waited for them to come and arrest him. While his friends slept, Jesus prayed that God would help him to bear what would happen next.

17. Read Mark's Gospel, chapter 15, verses 1 to 47

Here is a shortened version.

After Jesus was arrested, he was asked questions by Pilate. Even though he had done nothing wrong, the decision was that he should be crucified. Jesus was handed over to the Roman soldiers, who beat him. A crown of long, sharp thorns was put on his head, which dug into him.

They took Jesus to a place called Golgotha, which means 'The Place of the Skull'. He was very weak because they had beaten him so hard, so a man named Simon, who was from Cyrene, was forced to carry Jesus' cross.

Jesus was nailed to the cross. There were two criminals who were crucified on either side of him. There was a sign above Jesus that read, 'The King of the Jews'.

At about three o'clock in the afternoon, Jesus died.

His body was taken down from the cross, wrapped in cloths and placed in a tomb. A large, heavy stone was placed in front of the tomb.

'Good' Friday?

Good Friday is the day on which we remember that Jesus died on the cross. Children always ask why this day is called 'Good'. Some people say that it was originally 'God's Friday' and that the name we know developed from that. Another way of looking at it is to explain that although this was an awful day for Jesus, what he did was good for us. However, it is important to try to enter into the sadness and cruelty of this day in a way that is appropriate for you and your children, even if only for a short time. Today, the mood of Good Friday can be difficult to appreciate because in many ways it seems like any other day, but you will enter into the joy of Easter Day so much more if you have been able to experience something of the sadness of Good Friday.

Easter garden

In your Easter garden (see pages 22 and 23), roll the stone across the mouth of the tomb.

18. Hot cross buns

On Good Friday, you could buy hot cross buns together and **talk about** why we have a cross on the top. Although hot cross buns are in the shops for a long time before Good Friday, I suggest only having them on Good Friday, because this emphasises their significance.

As an alternative, you could buy plain, round biscuits and either draw a cross on the top using writing icing, or ice the top with a simple icing made by mixing icing sugar with a little water until thickened. Then make a cross with writing icing or by using small sweets or raisins.

19. Cross hunt

On Good Friday Jesus was nailed to a cross. Make crosses from lolly sticks using elastic bands to secure them. One person hides some around the home and other people have to find them. Who can find the most?

20. Silver hunt

The priests paid Judas 30 pieces of silver to betray Jesus. Look around the house. How many silver-coloured things can you find?

21. Good Friday word search

```
C R O W D F B P I V Y V M N R
T Z B D A Z M U K C J T T U G
D H B L I X U Y D O R E H O S
J I L T Y S E E X W H S X Z I
W U E C Q Z C N A I L S C D K
A Q L D Q G J I N E H X A W M
J V N X T P J N P V Z S V U U
F T L R W T O Z E L S C L S S
Z L I K R C V P S E E V B S Z
L A M X E Q M X B Q J S Q O N
L S W N Z C O D B M I M G R G
T M T X S Z L A T S G K E C Y
I S N T B B M I I F Z C K D F
O X G O A G I M U Z Q U O L Z
R A S R E B B O R T D Z B M D
```

CROSS   INNOCENT
CROWD   NAILS
DIED   ROBBERS
DISCIPLES   SAD
HEROD   TRIAL

43

Holy Week: Easter Saturday

The original Easter Saturday was a day when not much happened. Jesus had died and his friends could not go to the tomb until the following morning because of the Jewish Sabbath rules. It was a sad day for them, but it is an expectant one for us as we look forward to Easter Day. There are a few last-minute preparations that can be made.

Easter garden

Put the finishing touches to your Easter garden (see pages 22 and 23), perhaps adding some flowers.

22. Table decoration

Make a table decoration with a candle in the middle. Put some florist's foam in a plant pot, and push in some pieces of greenery. Put a candle in a pointed holder and push the point into the middle of the foam. Light the candle for your main meal on Easter Sunday in celebration of Jesus rising to new life.

23. Empty-tomb rolls

1. Use a packet bread-roll mix and make up the dough according to the recipe on the pack.

2. Wrap a tennis-ball-sized roll around a large marshmallow. Make sure that the marshmallow is sealed in by the dough.

3. Bake according to the instructions on the pack.

4. To test if the roll is cooked, tap it on the base. It should sound hollow.

5. When you open the roll, the marshmallow will have melted, leaving a hollow centre to represent the empty tomb... and leaving you with a warm, slightly sweet, freshly baked roll to enjoy!

Easter Day

On Easter Sunday Jesus' friends found that the stone blocking the tomb had been rolled away and his body was not there. He had risen from the dead! At first they were confused and some of them would not believe it, but soon they saw him for themselves.

24. Read John's Gospel, chapter 20, verses 1 to 10

On Sunday morning while it was still dark, Mary Magdalene went to the tomb and saw that the stone had been rolled away from the entrance. She ran to Simon Peter and to Jesus' favourite disciple and said,

'They have taken the Lord from the tomb! We don't know where they have put him.'

Peter and the other disciple started for the tomb. They ran side by side, until the other disciple ran faster than Peter and got there first. He bent over and saw the strips of linen cloth lying inside the tomb, but he did not go in.

When Simon Peter got there, he went into the tomb and saw the strips of cloth. He also saw the piece of cloth that had been used to cover Jesus' face. It was rolled up and in a place by itself. The disciple who got there first then went into the tomb, and when he saw it, he believed.

25. Easter egg hunt

Hide some small chocolate eggs around the house or in the garden. The rest of the family have to hunt around to find them.

Talk about why we have Easter eggs. The egg helps us to think about new life. The egg shape also helps us to think about the stone that was placed over the entrance to the tomb.

26. Easter egg throw

Buy some hollow plastic eggs and put a small chocolate egg inside each one to give them weight. Put a wicker basket or a bowl on the floor. Start close to the basket and toss an egg in. Keep moving back to see how far away you can be and still get the egg in the basket.

When you have gone as far back as you can, collect your eggs from the basket. Enjoy some of them together.

27. Edible nests

Mix together puffed rice cereal with melted chocolate. Make into a nest shape in a cake case. Add a few chocolate eggs to each one.

28. Wordmaker

Give each person or team a piece of paper with the words 'Easter celebration' on.

How many words of three letters or more can you make, using each letter only once?

Other words that could be used are:

Good Friday
Easter Sunday
Jesus is Risen

29. Easter Sunday word search

```
D Y F O C N J N E S I R D P U
W U Q T F J Z D O U O K R C S
M D O Q P V S Y A D N U S Z I
Y M X C U X Q T D U F O A S M
B K V N O U V E O D U G P R F
Z N D Q F O S N H N E X S C L
R I V N D I Q K O M E L B Q H
J N B H R F B M I S D B R U K
M R G P J F M M W V I C A B C
F Q R H S B K Q L L L L F F A
J U R N U C N B L O I C S F H
S E W H S V S P T V E M P T Y
D A L L E W H H E Y A K O W C
D N Q P J W Y D S U A I P A P
I V T U I E W X T W Q J R U F
```

ALIVE   STONE
CLOTH   SUNDAY
EMPTY   SURPRISED
JESUS   TOMB
RISEN

30. Jelly beans Easter poem

You will need a bag of different-coloured jelly beans and one cup per person for this activity. To make it easier, you can buy Jelly Belly® beans in individual colours from some shops.

Read this poem, allowing each person time to take a jelly bean of the matching colour and place it in their cup.

Red is for the blood he gave.
Green is for the grass he made.
Yellow is for the sunflowers so bright.
Black is for the dark of night.
White is for the grace he gave.
Orange is for the sun he made.
Purple is for the hours of sorrow.
Pink is for our new tomorrow.
A cup full of jelly beans, colourful and sweet.
It's a prayer, a promise, and everyone's treat.

Talk about what Easter means to your children again. Has their answer changed?

Further resources

On Easter Day in the Morning

Age range: 4–6s.

Mary has a friend called Jesus. Everywhere Jesus goes, special things happen. But one day soldiers march him away to die on a cross. Mary is very sad—until on Easter Day in the morning, something amazing happens. This is the perfect introduction to the events of the first Easter.

The Road to Easter Day

Age range: 5–7s.

'Along the road, along the road, the road to Easter Day...' Meet a young boy named Ben as he joins the crowds when Jesus enters Jerusalem on a donkey and continues along the road to Calvary. The journey ends at the garden tomb, where Ben discovers that the story is far from over...

Easter Days

Age range: 4–7s.

This activity book is based on the events leading up to the first Easter. From Jesus' entry into Jerusalem through to the resurrection, each part is illustrated with puzzles for all abilities.

You can view all our current Easter titles at our BRF Online Shop: www.brfonline.org.uk/easter-books.

Word search solutions

Good Friday:

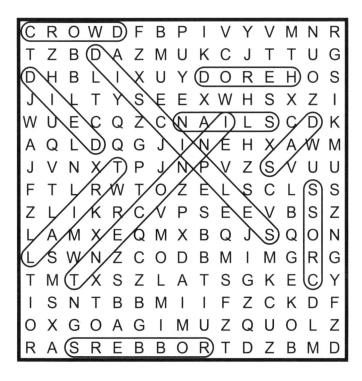

Easter Sunday:

```
D Y F O C N J N E S I R D P U
W U Q T F J Z D O U O K R C S
M D O Q P V S Y A D N U S Z I
Y M X C U X Q T D U F O A S M
B K V N O U V E O D U G P R F
Z N D Q F O S N H N E X S C L
R I V N D I Q K O M E L B Q H
J N B H R F B M I S D B R U K
M R G P J F M M W V I C A B C
F Q R H S B K Q L L L L F F A
J U R N U C N B L O I C S F H
S E W H S V S P T V E M P T Y
D A L L E W H H E Y A K O W C
D N Q P J W Y D S U A I P A P
I V T U I E W X T W Q J R U F
```

Index of activities

About Faith in Homes

www.faithinhomes.org.uk

The Faith in Homes ministry includes three elements—resourcing, researching and signposting.

Resourcing

Living out the Christian faith at home may not seem easy for families. Our hope is that you will find the Faith in Homes website a place of easy-to-use ideas, resources, events and links to other websites to help you live out your faith together. The Barnabas Children's Ministry Team is passionate about finding a variety of ways to encourage and support all families.

This website is also for church leaders who share our vision of helping to nurture faith in the home. We offer a wide range of relevant articles, publications and research, as well as support and practical ways for churches to encourage faith within the home.

Researching

Alongside all of this, we are actively researching new ways and approaches to support faith within the home. We are asking questions such as:

What is needed to encourage and resource faith to happen or develop further in the home?

What are the challenges faced?

How can 'church' and 'home' work together to support families?

The answers to these and other questions will enable us to meet the needs of families of all styles and backgrounds.

Signposting

In addition to all the material available on the Faith in Homes website, you will also find links to resources, events, organisations and other websites that may be of interest.

About the author

Jane Butcher is responsible for developing the Faith in Homes ministry, which is something for which she has a passion and vision, both as a member of the Barnabas Children's Ministry Team and as a parent. She has a desire that parents, church leaders and others share in this ministry and feel encouraged, supported and resourced to engage with such an important area.

Jane originally trained and worked as a teacher, but moved into church ministry in 1993. She has a wide range of experience in schools and churches from her posts in both the UK and USA. She has led training sessions and seminars in a variety of schools, churches and dioceses on many different aspects of RE and children's ministry, and is also an accredited Godly Play Teacher.

Enjoyed

this book?

Write a review—we'd love to hear what you think.
Email: reviews@brf.org.uk

Keep up to date—receive details of our new books as they happen.
Sign up for email news and select your interest groups at:
www.brfonline.org.uk/findoutmore/

Follow us on Twitter @brfonline

By post—to receive new title information by post (UK only), complete the form below and post to: BRF Mailing Lists, 15 The Chambers, Vineyard, Abingdon, Oxfordshire, OX14 3FE

Your Details
Name _____
Address_____
_____
Town/City _____ Post Code _____
Email _____

Your Interest Groups (*Please tick as appropriate)	
❏ Advent/Lent	❏ Messy Church
❏ Bible Reading & Study	❏ Pastoral
❏ Children's Books	❏ Prayer & Spirituality
❏ Discipleship	❏ Resources for Children's Church
❏ Leadership	❏ Resources for Schools

Support your local bookshop
Ask about their new title information schemes.